For Andrew

First published 1999 by Walker Books Ltd
87 Vauxhall Walk, London SE11 5HJ

2 4 6 8 10 9 7 5 3 1

© 1999 Vanessa Cabban

This book has been typeset in Horley Old Style.

Printed in Hong Kong

British Library Cataloguing in Publication Data
A catalogue record for this book is
available from the British Library.

ISBN 0-7445-6155-8 (hb)
ISBN 0-7445-6786-6 (pb)

Bertie and Small

and the Brave Sea Journey

Vanessa Cabban

WALKER BOOKS
AND SUBSIDIARIES
LONDON · BOSTON · SYDNEY

Bertie and Small
play together every day.

Small is the rabbit and Bertie
wears the hat with long floppy ears.

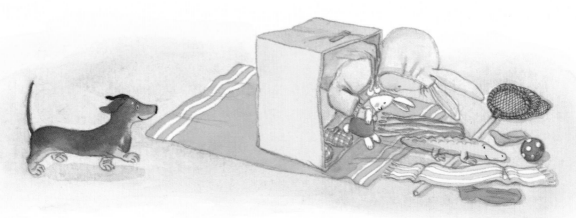

Bertie and Small make a house

but it's not big enough
and it's too hot.

"Oops!" says Bertie.

Bertie takes Small for a car ride.
Vroom! Vroom! Vroom!

Bertie hides inside the
box with Small.

"Let's sail across the sea," says Bertie.
"Watch out for sea-snakes."

A storm comes and
the boat shivers and shakes.

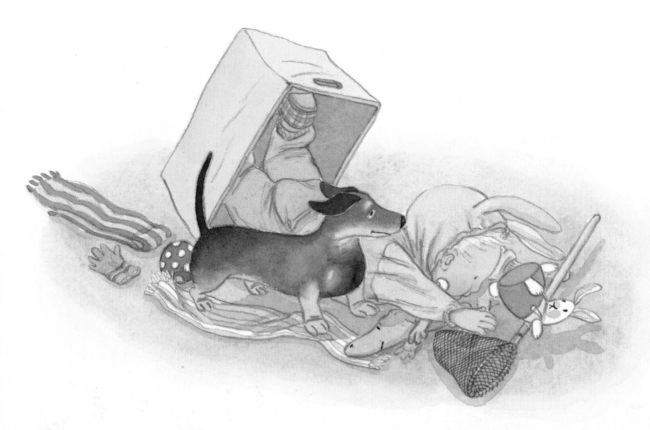

Small falls overboard and Bertie
tumbles out behind him.

"Youch!" says Bertie.

But Bertie is clever and Small is brave
and they save each other.

And then Daddy comes.

"Play with us, Daddy," says Bertie.

Daddy is the ship's engineer and
Bertie and Small are the navigators.

They say Boo! to the crocodile
and Huh! to the sea-snakes.

Then Bertie and Small
and Daddy go ashore for a drink.

"The storm was rough," says Bertie.
"Small was really brave."